fresh

barbecues
&salads

fresh

barbecues
& salads

Marks and Spencer p.l.c.
PO Box 3339
Chester, CH99 9QS

www.marksandspencer.com

ISBN: 1-84461-285-6

Printed in Singapore

This edition designed by Shelley Doyle

Photography and text by The Bridgewater Book Company Ltd

Cover Photography by Mark Wood

Cover Home Economist Pamela Gwyther

NOTES FOR THE READER

This book uses both metric and imperial measurements. Follow the same units of measurement throughout; do not mix metric and imperial.

All spoon measurements are level: teaspoons are assumed to be 5 ml, and tablespoons are assumed to be 15 ml.

Unless otherwise stated, milk is assumed to be full fat and eggs are medium.

Recipes using raw or very lightly cooked eggs should be avoided by infants, the elderly, pregnant women, convalescents and anyone suffering from an illness.

Optional ingredients, variations or serving suggestions have not been included in the calculations. The times given are an approximate guide only. Preparation times differ according to the techniques used by different people and the cooking times may also vary from those given.

contents

Introduction

There's something about eating outdoors that sharpens the appetite and heightens the senses, making us more aware of the colours, flavours, textures and aromas of the food on our plates. The barbecue is the essence of summer eating, whether for family meals or entertaining guests. It is fundamentally a very primitive cooking technique, even though nowadays all kinds of sophisticated extras, from rotating spits to fingertip heat controls, are available. For these reasons, the freshness and flavour of what we are grilling become even more important. Of course, marinades and sauces are an integral part of a barbecue meal, but they are always intended to enhance, not disguise, the flavour of the main ingredient.

Food for barbecues should be treated with care. If meat or fish is to be marinated for less than an hour, it can be left to stand in a cool place in the kitchen. Otherwise, it is best to marinate in the refrigerator and, in both cases, cover the dish with clingfilm. Don't transfer food outdoors until you are ready to cook and keep raw and cooked food – and the utensils you use for each – quite separate. Don't leave dips, sauces, dressings and mayonnaise baking in the hot sunshine and exposed to flies.

As far as salads are concerned, freshness is everything. Salad leaves should be full of colour and crisp, vegetables should have 'bite' and fruit should be juicy. Don't add dressings much in advance of serving as this will result in a disappointing, soggy mess rather than what should be a refreshing, palate-cleansing delight.

Meat & Poultry

The crowning glory of any barbecue should be the freshest and most succulent meat & poultry available. The highest quality ingredients will speak for themselves, with simple sauces and dressings, producing dishes such as Tabasco Steak with Watercress Butter or Chicken Satay Skewers with Lime.

thai-spiced beef & pepper kebabs

MARINADE

2 tbsp sherry

2 tbsp rice wine

75 ml/2½ fl oz soy sauce

75 ml/2½ fl oz hoisin sauce

3 cloves garlic, finely chopped

1 red chilli, deseeded and finely chopped

1½ tbsp grated fresh root ginger

3 spring onions, trimmed and finely chopped

salt and pepper

KEBABS

1 kg/2 lb 4 oz rump or sirloin steak, cubed

2 large red peppers, deseeded and cut into small chunks

green and red lettuce leaves, to serve

very easy - serves 4

Put the sherry, rice wine, soy sauce, hoisin sauce, garlic, chilli, ginger and spring onions into a large bowl and mix until well combined. Season to taste.

Thread the meat onto 8 skewers, alternating it with chunks of red pepper. When the skewers are full (leave a small space at either end), transfer them to the bowl and turn them in the soy sauce mixture until they are well coated. Cover with clingfilm and place in the refrigerator to marinate for at least 2½ hours or overnight.

When the skewers are thoroughly marinated, lift them out and barbecue them over hot coals, turning them frequently, for 10–15 minutes or until the meat is cooked right through. Serve at once on a bed of green and red lettuce leaves.

650 g/1 lb 7 oz minced beef

1 red pepper, deseeded and finely chopped

1 garlic clove, finely chopped

2 small red chillies, deseeded and finely chopped

1 tbsp chopped fresh basil

1/2 tsp powdered cumin

salt and pepper

sprigs of fresh basil, to garnish

hamburger buns, to serve

very easy — serves 4

Put the minced beef, red pepper, garlic, chillies, chopped basil and cumin into a bowl and mix until well combined. Season with salt and pepper.

Using your hands, form the mixture into burger shapes. Barbecue the burgers over hot coals for 5–8 minutes on each side or until cooked right through. Garnish with sprigs of basil and serve with hamburger buns.

beefburgers with chilli & basil

tabasco **steaks** with watercress butter

1 bunch of watercress

85 g/3 oz unsalted butter, softened

4 sirloin steaks, about 225 g/8 oz each

4 tsp Tabasco sauce

salt and pepper

very easy – serves 4

Preheat the barbecue. Using a sharp knife, finely chop enough watercress to fill 4 tablespoons. Reserve a few watercress leaves for the garnish. Place the butter in a small bowl and beat in the chopped watercress with a fork until fully incorporated. Cover with clingfilm and leave to chill in the refrigerator until required.

Sprinkle each steak with 1 teaspoon of the Tabasco sauce, rubbing it in well. Season to taste with salt and pepper.

Cook the steaks over hot coals for 2½ minutes each side for rare, 4 minutes each side for medium and 6 minutes each side for well done. Transfer to serving plates, garnish with the reserved watercress leaves and serve immediately, topped with the watercress butter.

hot & spicy ribs

1 onion, chopped

2 garlic cloves, chopped

2.5-cm/1- inch piece fresh root ginger, sliced

1 fresh red chilli, deseeded and chopped

5 tbsp dark soy sauce

3 tbsp lime juice

1 tbsp palm or muscovado sugar

2 tbsp groundnut oil

salt and pepper

1 kg/2 lb 4 oz pork spare ribs, separated

easy - serves 4

Preheat the barbecue. Put the onion, garlic, ginger, chilli and soy sauce into a food processor and process to a paste. Transfer to a jug and stir in the lime juice, sugar and oil and season to taste with salt and pepper.

Place the spare ribs in a preheated wok or large, heavy-based saucepan and pour in the soy sauce mixture. Place on the hob and bring to the boil, then simmer over a low heat, stirring frequently, for 30 minutes. If the mixture appears to be drying out, add a little water.

Remove the spare ribs, reserving the sauce. Cook the ribs over medium hot coals, turning and basting frequently with the sauce, for 20–30 minutes. Transfer to a large serving plate and serve immediately.

barbecued pork sausages with thyme

1 garlic clove, finely chopped

1 onion, grated

1 small red chilli, deseeded and finely chopped

450 g/1 lb lean minced pork

50 g/1¾ oz almonds, toasted and ground

50 g/1¾ oz fresh breadcrumbs

1 tbsp finely chopped fresh thyme

salt and pepper

flour, for dusting

vegetable oil, for brushing

fresh finger rolls, slices of onion, lightly cooked, and tomato ketchup and/or mustard to serve

very easy – serves 4

Put the garlic, onion, chilli, pork, almonds, breadcrumbs and fresh thyme into a large bowl. Season well with salt and pepper and mix until well combined.

Using your hands, form the mixture into sausage shapes. Roll each sausage in a little flour, then transfer to a bowl, cover with clingfilm and refrigerate for 45 minutes.

Brush a piece of aluminium foil with oil, then put the sausages on the foil and brush them with a little more vegetable oil. Transfer the sausages and foil to the barbecue. Barbecue over hot coals, turning the sausages frequently, for about 15 minutes or until cooked right through. Serve with finger rolls, cooked sliced onion and tomato ketchup and/or mustard.

MARINADE

2 tsp vegetable oil

1 tsp curry powder

1 tsp garam masala

2 tsp granulated sugar

200 ml/7fl oz natural yogurt

SKEWERS

400 g/14 oz boneless lamb, cubed

140 g/5 oz dried apricot halves

1 red or green pepper, deseeded and cut into small chunks

2 courgettes, cubed

16 baby onions

fresh coriander leaves, to garnish

freshly steamed or boiled rice and crisp green salad leaves to serve

very easy - serves 4

Put the oil, spices, sugar and yogurt into a large bowl and mix until well combined.

Thread the lamb onto 8 skewers, alternating it with the apricot halves, red or green pepper, courgettes and baby onions. When the skewers are full (leave a small space at either end), transfer them to the bowl and turn them in the yogurt mixture until they are well coated. Cover with clingfilm and place in the refrigerator to marinate for at least 8 hours or overnight.

When the skewers are thoroughly marinated, lift them out and barbecue them over hot coals, turning them frequently, for 15 minutes or until the meat is cooked right through. Serve at once with freshly cooked rice or a crisp green salad, garnished with fresh coriander leaves.

curried lamb skewers

turkey with coriander pesto

450 g/1 lb skinless, boneless turkey, cut into
   5-cm/2-inch cubes

2 courgettes, thickly sliced

1 red and 1 yellow pepper, deseeded and cut into
   5-cm/2-inch squares

8 cherry tomatoes

8 baby onions

MARINADE

6 tbsp olive oil

3 tbsp dry white wine

1 tsp green peppercorns, crushed

2 tbsp chopped fresh coriander

salt

CORIANDER PESTO

55 g/2 oz fresh coriander leaves

15 g/1/2 oz fresh parsley leaves

1 garlic clove

55 g/2 oz pine kernels

25 g/1 oz freshly grated Parmesan cheese

6 tbsp extra-virgin olive oil

juice of 1 lemon

easy – serves 4

Place the turkey in a large glass bowl. To make the marinade, mix the olive oil, wine, peppercorns and coriander together in a jug and season to taste with salt. Pour the mixture over the turkey and turn until the turkey is thoroughly coated. Cover with clingfilm and leave to marinate in the refrigerator for 2 hours.

Preheat the barbecue. To make the pesto, put the coriander and parsley into a food processor and process until finely chopped. Add the garlic and pine kernels and pulse until chopped. Add the Parmesan cheese, oil and lemon juice and process briefly to mix. Transfer to a bowl, cover and leave to chill in the refrigerator until required.

Drain the turkey, reserving the marinade. Thread the turkey, courgette slices, pepper pieces, cherry tomatoes and onions alternately onto metal skewers. Cook over medium hot coals, turning and brushing frequently with the marinade, for 10 minutes. Serve immediately with the coriander pesto.

blackened chicken

4 skinless, boneless whole chicken breasts, about
   175 g/6 oz each

2 tbsp natural yogurt

1 tbsp lemon juice

1 garlic clove, very finely chopped

1 tsp paprika

1 tsp ground cumin

1 tsp mustard powder

$\frac{1}{2}$ tsp dried thyme

$\frac{1}{2}$ tsp dried oregano

$\frac{1}{2}$ tsp cayenne pepper

sunflower oil, for brushing

thinly sliced onion rings, to garnish

easy - serves 4

Preheat the barbecue. Using a sharp knife, slice the chicken breasts in half horizontally and flatten them slightly with your hand. Place the chicken pieces in a large, shallow, non-metallic dish. Mix the yogurt and lemon juice together in a small bowl and brush the mixture all over the chicken.

Mix the garlic, paprika, cumin, mustard powder, thyme, oregano and cayenne together in a separate bowl and sprinkle the mixture evenly over the chicken.

Brush the chicken pieces with oil and cook over medium hot coals for 3 minutes on each side, or until beginning to blacken and the chicken is thoroughly cooked. Transfer to a large serving plate and garnish with thinly sliced onion rings. Serve immediately.

sweet & sour chicken wings

MARINADE

2 tbsp sweet sherry

3 tbsp sherry vinegar or red wine vinegar

4 tbsp soy sauce

200 ml/7 fl oz orange juice

100 ml/$3\frac{1}{2}$ fl oz chicken stock or vegetable stock

50 g/$1\frac{3}{4}$ oz brown sugar

pepper

1 tbsp tomato purée

2 garlic cloves, finely chopped

1 red chilli, deseeded and chopped

CHICKEN

1.8 kg/4 lb chicken wings

wedges of oranges and 1 long, red chilli, made into
  a flower (see below)

very easy – serves 4

Put the sherry, vinegar, soy sauce, orange juice, stock and sugar into a food processor and season well. Blend until combined. Add the tomato purée, garlic and chilli and blend until smooth. Separate the chicken wings at the joints and put them into a non-metallic (glass or ceramic) bowl, which will not react with acid. Pour over enough marinade to cover the chicken, cover with clingfilm and refrigerate for at least $2\frac{1}{2}$ hours. Cover the remaining marinade with clingfilm and refrigerate until the chicken is ready.

When the chicken wings are thoroughly marinated, lift them out and barbecue them over hot coals for about 20 minutes, turning them frequently and basting with the remaining marinade. Cut into a thick part of a wing to check that the chicken is cooked all the way through. If it is still pink in the middle, continue to cook until the chicken is thoroughly cooked. Garnish with orange wedges and a chilli flower (made by making 1-cm/$\frac{1}{2}$-inch slits in a chilli and soaking in iced water for 30 minutes until fanned out).

MARINADE

100 ml/3½ fl oz soy sauce

100 ml/3½ fl oz lime juice

2 tbsp smooth peanut butter

2 tbsp garam masala

1 tbsp brown sugar

2 garlic cloves, finely chopped

1 small red chilli, deseeded and finely chopped

pepper

SKEWERS

6 skinless, boneless chicken breasts, cubed

fresh coriander leaves, shredded and wedges
   of lime to garnish

freshly steamed or boiled rice, or crisp green
   salad leaves, to serve

extremely easy - serves 4

Put the soy sauce, lime juice, peanut butter, garam masala, sugar, garlic and chilli into a large bowl and mix until well combined. Season with plenty of pepper.

Thread the chicken cubes onto skewers (leave a small space at either end). Transfer them to the bowl and turn them in the peanut butter mixture until they are well coated. Cover with clingfilm and place in the refrigerator to marinate for at least 2½ hours.

When the skewers are thoroughly marinated, lift them out and barbecue them over hot coals for 15 minutes or until cooked right through, turning them frequently and basting with the remaining marinade. Arrange the skewers on a bed of freshly cooked rice or crisp green salad leaves, garnish with coriander leaves and lime wedges and serve.

chicken satay skewers with lime

Fish & Seafood

Fish and seafood barbecue dishes offer a great alternative to meat and allow you to sample the delights of fresh sea fare with the minimum of effort. With dishes like sumptuous Chargrilled Tuna with Chilli Salsa, or sizzling Oriental Prawn Skewers, the very best fish and seafood can take centre stage.

surf &
turf
kebabs

FISH KEBABS

12 raw tiger prawns
4 shallots, halved
12 cherry tomatoes
2 tbsp sunflower oil
$1/2$ tsp ground coriander
pepper

STEAK KEBABS

400 g/14 oz rump steak, cut into 2.5-cm/1-inch
    cubes
4 onions, quartered
8 bay leaves
2 tbsp sunflower oil
$1/2$–$3/4$ tsp chilli powder

CHICKEN KEBABS

400 g/14 oz skinless, boneless chicken breasts,
    cut into 2.5-cm/1-inch cubes
2 courgettes, thickly sliced
2 fresh pineapple slices, cut into cubes
2 tbsp sunflower oil
2 tbsp dark soy sauce
2 tbsp redcurrant jelly
pepper

easy – serves 4

Preheat the barbecue. Remove the heads from the prawns. Thread the shallots, prawns and cherry tomatoes alternately onto 4 metal skewers. Thread the steak, onion quarters and bay leaves alternately onto 4 metal skewers. Thread the chicken, courgette slices and pineapple cubes alternately onto 4 metal skewers.

For the prawn kebabs, mix the oil and ground coriander together in a small bowl and season to taste with pepper, then brush all over the kebabs. For the steak kebabs, mix the oil and chilli powder to taste in a separate bowl, then brush all over the kebabs. For the

chicken kebabs, mix the oil, soy sauce and redcurrant jelly together in a third bowl and season to taste with pepper, then brush all over the kebabs.

Cook the prawn kebabs over medium hot coals, turning frequently and brushing with any remaining coriander-flavoured oil, for 6–8 minutes. Cook the steak kebabs on the hottest part of the barbecue, turning frequently and brushing with any remaining chilli-flavoured oil, for 5–8 minutes. Cook the chicken kebabs over medium hot coals for 6–10 minutes, turning frequently and brushing with any remaining soy-flavoured oil. Serve when the kebabs are all cooked.

MARINADE

100 ml/3¹/₂ fl oz vegetable oil

2 tbsp chilli oil

50 ml/2 fl oz lemon juice

1 tbsp rice wine or sherry

2 spring onions, trimmed and finely chopped

2 garlic cloves, finely chopped

1 tbsp grated fresh root ginger

1 tbsp chopped fresh lemon-grass

2 tbsp chopped fresh coriander

salt and pepper

SKEWERS

1 kg/2 lb 4 oz large prawns, peeled and deveined,
   but with tails left on

wedges of lemon and chopped fresh chives
   to garnish

freshly cooked jasmine rice, to serve

very easy – serves 4

Put the oils, lemon juice, rice wine, spring onions, garlic, ginger, lemon-grass and coriander into a food processor and season well with salt and pepper. Process until smooth, then transfer to a non-metallic (glass or ceramic) bowl, which will not react with acid.

Add the prawns to the bowl and turn them in the mixture until they are well coated. Cover with clingfilm and place in the refrigerator to marinate for at least 2 hours.

When the prawns are thoroughly marinated, lift them out and thread them onto skewers leaving a small space at either end. Barbecue them with the lemon wedges over hot coals for 4–5 minutes or until cooked right through (but do not overcook), turning them frequently and basting with the remaining marinade. Arrange the skewers on a bed of freshly cooked jasmine rice, garnish with the lemon wedges and chopped fresh chives.

oriental prawn skewers

monkfish skewers with courgettes & lemon

450 g/1 lb monkfish tail

2 courgettes

1 lemon

12 cherry tomatoes

8 bay leaves

4 tbsp olive oil

2 tbsp lemon juice

1 tsp chopped fresh thyme

$\frac{1}{2}$ tsp lemon pepper

salt

green salad leaves and fresh crusty bread to serve

very easy – serves 4

Preheat the barbecue. Using a sharp knife, cut the monkfish into 5-cm/2-inch chunks. Cut the courgettes into thick slices and the lemon into wedges.

Thread the monkfish, courgettes, lemon, tomatoes and bay leaves onto 4 metal skewers.

Mix the olive oil, lemon juice, thyme, lemon pepper and salt to taste together in a small bowl, then brush liberally all over the fish, lemon, tomatoes and bay leaves on the skewers.

Cook the skewers over medium hot coals for 15 minutes, basting frequently with the remaining oil mixture. Serve the skewers with green salad leaves and plenty of fresh crusty bread.

chargrilled **tuna** with chilli salsa

4 tuna steaks, about 175 g/6 oz each

grated rind and juice of 1 lime

2 tbsp olive oil

salt and pepper

fresh coriander sprigs, to garnish

CHILLI SALSA

2 orange peppers

1 tbsp olive oil

juice of 1 lime

juice of 1 orange

2–3 fresh red chillies, deseeded and chopped

pinch of cayenne pepper

easy – serves 4

Rinse the tuna thoroughly under cold running water and pat dry with kitchen paper, then place in a large, shallow, non-metallic dish. Sprinkle the lime rind and juice and the olive oil over the fish. Season to taste with salt and pepper, cover with clingfilm and leave to marinate in the refrigerator for up to 1 hour.

Preheat the barbecue. To make the salsa, brush the peppers with the olive oil and cook over hot coals, turning frequently, for 10 minutes, or until the skin is blackened and charred. Remove from the barbecue and leave to cool slightly, then peel off the skins and discard the seeds. Put the peppers into a food processor with the remaining salsa ingredients and process to a purée. Transfer to a bowl and season to taste with salt and pepper.

Cook the tuna over hot coals for 4–5 minutes on each side, until golden. Transfer to serving plates, garnish with coriander sprigs and serve with the salsa.

4 cod steaks, about 175 g/6 oz each

2 tsp extra-virgin olive oil

4 tomatoes, peeled and chopped

25 g/1 oz fresh basil leaves, torn into small pieces

4 tbsp white wine

salt and pepper

cod & tomato parcels

very easy - serves 4

Preheat the barbecue. Rinse the cod steaks under cold running water and pat dry with kitchen paper. Using a sharp knife, cut out and discard the central bones. Cut out 4 rectangles, 33 x 20 cm/13 x 8 inches, from double-thickness foil and brush with the olive oil. Place a cod steak in the centre of each piece of foil.

Mix the tomatoes, basil and white wine together in a bowl and season to taste with salt and pepper. Spoon the tomato mixture equally on top of the fish. Bring up the sides of the foil and fold over securely.

Cook the cod parcels over hot coals for 3–5 minutes on each side. Transfer to 4 large serving plates and serve immediately in the parcels.

MARINADE

2 tbsp white wine

3 tbsp balsamic vinegar

1 tbsp extra-virgin olive oil

1 garlic clove, finely chopped

salt and pepper

SKEWERS

300 g/10$\frac{1}{2}$ oz fresh tuna steaks

450 g/1 lb button mushrooms

chopped fresh tarragon, to garnish

freshly cooked rice and mixed salad to serve

extremely easy – serves 4

Put the wine, vinegar, olive oil and garlic into a large bowl and mix until well combined. Season with salt and pepper to taste.

Rinse the tuna steaks under cold running water and pat dry with kitchen paper. Cut them into small cubes. Wipe the mushrooms clean with kitchen paper. Thread the tuna cubes onto skewers, alternating them with the button mushrooms. When the skewers are full (leave a small space at either end), transfer them to the bowl and turn them in the wine mixture until they are well coated. Cover with clingfilm and place in the refrigerator to marinate for at least 30 minutes.

Barbecue the skewers over hot coals for about 10 minutes or until the tuna is cooked right through (but do not overcook), turning them frequently and basting with the remaining marinade. Arrange the skewers on a bed of rice, garnish with chopped fresh tarragon and serve with a mixed salad.

tuna & tarragon skewers

baked red mullet

4 banana leaves

2 limes

3 garlic cloves

4 red mullet, about 350 g/12 oz each

2 spring onions, thinly sliced

2.5-cm/1-inch piece fresh root ginger

1 onion, finely chopped

4¹⁄₂ tsp groundnut or corn oil

3 tbsp kecap manis or light soy sauce

1 tsp ground coriander

1 tsp ground cumin

¹⁄₄ tsp ground cloves

¹⁄₄ tsp ground turmeric

easy - serves 4

Preheat the barbecue. If necessary, cut the banana leaves into 4 x 40-cm/16-inch squares, using a sharp knife or scissors. Thinly slice ¹⁄₂ a lime and 1 garlic clove. Clean and scale the fish, then rinse it inside and out under cold running water. Pat dry with kitchen paper. Using a sharp knife, make a series of deep diagonal slashes on the side of each fish, then insert the lime and garlic slices into the slashes. Place the fish on the banana leaf squares and sprinkle with the spring onions.

Finely chop the remaining garlic and squeeze the juice from the remaining limes. Finely chop the ginger, then place the garlic in a bowl with the onion, ginger, oil, kecap manis, spices and lime juice and mix to a paste.

Spoon the paste into the fish cavities and spread it over the outside. Roll up the parcels and tie securely with string. Cook over medium hot coals, turning occasionally, for 15–20 minutes. Serve.

charred **fish**

4 white fish steaks

1 tbsp paprika

1 tsp dried thyme

1 tsp cayenne pepper

1 tsp black pepper

$1/2$ tsp white pepper

$1/2$ tsp salt

$1/4$ tsp ground allspice

50 g/$1^3/4$ oz unsalted butter

3 tbsp sunflower oil

very easy – serves 4

Preheat the barbecue. Rinse the fish steaks under cold running water and pat dry with kitchen paper.

Mix the paprika, thyme, cayenne, black and white pepper, salt and allspice together in a shallow dish.

Place the butter and sunflower oil in a small saucepan and heat gently, stirring occasionally, until the butter melts.

Brush the butter mixture liberally all over the fish steaks, on both sides, then dip the fish into the spicy mix until coated on both sides.

Cook the fish over hot coals for 3 minutes, on each side until cooked through. Continue to baste the fish with the remaining butter mixture during the cooking time.

100 ml/3½ fl oz vegetable oil

100 ml/3½ fl oz dry white wine

1 tbsp black treacle

1 tbsp brown sugar

1 tbsp soy sauce

1 garlic clove, chopped

pinch of mixed spice

salt and pepper

4 salmon steaks, about 200 g/7 oz each

barbecued
salmon

wedges of lemon, to garnish

crisp green salad leaves, to serve

extremely easy – serves 4

Put the oil, wine, black treacle, sugar, soy sauce, garlic and mixed spice into a large bowl and mix until well combined. Season with salt and pepper.

Rinse the salmon steaks under cold running water, then pat dry with kitchen paper. Add them to the wine mixture and turn them until they are well coated. Cover with clingfilm and place in the refrigerator to marinate for at least 2 hours or overnight.

When the steaks are thoroughly marinated, lift them out and barbecue them over hot coals for about 10 minutes on each side or until cooked right through, turning them frequently and basting with the remaining marinade. About halfway through the cooking time, add the lemon wedges and barbecue for 4–5 minutes, turning once. Arrange the steaks on a bed of fresh green salad leaves, garnish with the lemon wedges, and serve.

1.5 kg/3 lb 5 oz sea bass, cleaned and scaled

1–2 tsp olive oil

1 tsp saffron powder

salt and pepper

½ lemon, sliced, plus extra to garnish

1 lime, sliced, plus extra to garnish

1 bunch of fresh thyme

easy – serves 6

Preheat the barbecue. Rinse the sea bass inside and out under cold running water, then pat dry with kitchen paper. Using a sharp knife, make a series of shallow diagonal slashes along each side of the fish. Brush each slash with a little olive oil, then sprinkle over the saffron powder.

Brush a large fish basket with olive oil and place the fish in the basket, but do not close it. Season the cavity with salt and pepper. Place the lemon and lime slices and the thyme in the cavity without overfilling it.

Close the basket and cook the fish over medium hot coals for 10 minutes on each side. Carefully transfer to a large serving plate, garnish with lemon and lime slices and serve immediately.

caribbean sea bass

Vegetarian & Salads

Glistening fresh vegetables and crisp vibrant salads can transform a barbecue into a feast. Gorgeous Haloumi Cheese and Vegetable Kebabs add an element of sophistication, and fresh ingredients in an Avocado, Sweetcorn and Walnut Salad provide the most heavenly of accompaniments.

bean & vegetable burgers with tomato salsa

BURGERS

200 g/7 oz canned chickpeas, drained and rinsed

200 g/7 oz canned cannellini beans, drained and rinsed

1 large courgette, finely grated

1 large carrot, peeled and finely grated

1 garlic clove, peeled and finely chopped

85 g/3 oz breadcrumbs

salt and pepper

SALSA

4 large tomatoes, chopped

1 tbsp lime juice

2 shallots, peeled and chopped

1 garlic clove, peeled and chopped

1 tbsp chopped fresh basil

chopped fresh basil and wedges of lime to garnish

hamburger buns, to serve

very easy - serves 4

Put the chickpeas and cannellini beans into a food processor and blend together briefly. Transfer to a large bowl, then add the courgette, carrot, garlic and breadcrumbs. Season with salt and pepper, then mix together until thoroughly combined. Using your hands, form the mixture into burger shapes, transfer to a shallow dish and cover with clingfilm. Refrigerate for 30 minutes.

To make the salsa, put the tomatoes, lime juice, shallots, garlic and basil into a bowl and stir together. Cover with clingfilm and set aside.

Barbecue the burgers over hot coals for 5–10 minutes on each side or until cooked right through. Remove from the coals and transfer to serving plates. Garnish with chopped basil and wedges of lime and serve with hamburger buns and the salsa.

MARINADE

4 tbsp extra-virgin olive oil

2 tbsp balsamic vinegar

2 garlic cloves, finely chopped

1 tbsp chopped fresh coriander

salt and pepper

KEBABS

225 g/8 oz haloumi cheese

12 button mushrooms

8 baby onions

12 cherry tomatoes

2 courgettes, cut into small chunks

1 red pepper, deseeded and cut into small chunks

chopped fresh coriander, to garnish

freshly cooked rice or salad leaves and fresh crusty
  bread to serve

very easy – serves 4

Put the oil, vinegar, garlic and coriander into a large bowl. Season with salt and pepper and mix until well combined.

Cut the haloumi cheese into bite-sized cubes. Thread the cubes onto skewers, alternating them with whole button mushrooms, baby onions, cherry tomatoes, and courgette and red pepper chunks. When the skewers are full (leave a small space at either end), transfer them to the bowl and turn them in the mixture until they are well coated. Cover with clingfilm

and place in the refrigerator to marinate for at least 2 hours.

When the skewers are thoroughly marinated, barbecue them over hot coals for 5–10 minutes or until they are cooked to your taste, turning them frequently and basting with the remaining marinade. Arrange the skewers on a bed of freshly cooked rice or fresh mixed salad leaves, garnish with coriander leaves and serve with fresh crusty bread.

haloumi cheese & vegetable kebabs

spicy **sweet potato** slices

450 g/1 lb sweet potatoes
2 tbsp sunflower oil
1 tsp chilli sauce
salt and pepper

very easy - serves 4

Preheat the barbecue. Bring a large saucepan of water to the boil. Add the sweet potatoes and parboil them for 10 minutes. Drain thoroughly and transfer to a chopping board. Allow to cool. Peel the potatoes and cut them into thick slices.

Mix the sunflower oil, chilli sauce and salt and pepper to taste together in a small bowl. Brush the spicy mixture liberally over one side of the potatoes. Place the potatoes, oil-side down, over medium hot coals and cook for 5–6 minutes.

Lightly brush the tops of the potatoes with the oil, turn them over and barbecue for a further 5 minutes, or until crisp and golden. Transfer the potatoes to a warmed serving dish and serve immediately.

pumpkin parcels

700 g/1 lb 9 oz pumpkin or squash

2 tbsp sunflower oil

25 g/1 oz butter

1/2 tsp chilli sauce

grated rind of 1 lime

2 tsp lime juice

very easy – serves 4

Preheat the barbecue. Halve the pumpkin or squash and scoop out the seeds. Rinse the seeds and reserve. Cut the pumpkin into thin wedges and peel.

Heat the sunflower oil and butter together in a large saucepan, stirring, until melted. Stir in the chilli sauce, lime rind and juice.

Add the pumpkin and seeds to the saucepan and toss to coat on all sides in the flavoured butter.

Divide the mixture between 4 double-thickness sheets of foil. Fold over the foil to enclose the pumpkin mixture completely.

Cook the foil parcels over hot coals for 15–25 minutes, or until the pumpkin is tender. Transfer the foil parcels to warmed serving plates. Open the parcels at the table and serve immediately.

spicy vegetarian sausages

1 garlic clove, finely chopped

1 onion, finely chopped

1 red chilli, deseeded and finely chopped

400 g/14 oz canned red kidney beans, rinsed, drained and mashed

100 g/3$\frac{1}{2}$ oz fresh breadcrumbs

50 g/1$\frac{3}{4}$ oz almonds, toasted and ground

50 g/1$\frac{3}{4}$ oz cooked rice

50 g/1$\frac{3}{4}$ oz Cheddar cheese, grated

1 egg yolk

1 tbsp chopped fresh oregano

salt and pepper

flour, for dusting

vegetable oil, for brushing

fresh finger rolls, slices of onion, lightly cooked and tomato ketchup and/or mustard to serve

easy – serves 4

Put the garlic, onion, chilli, mashed kidney beans, breadcrumbs, almonds, rice and cheese into a large bowl. Stir in the egg yolk and oregano, then season with salt and plenty of pepper.

Using your hands, form the mixture into sausage shapes. Roll each sausage in a little flour, then transfer to a bowl, cover with clingfilm and refrigerate for 45 minutes.

Brush a piece of aluminium foil with oil, then put the sausages on the foil and brush them with a little more vegetable oil. Transfer the sausages and foil to the barbecue. Barbecue over hot coals, turning the sausages frequently, for about 15 minutes or until cooked right through. Serve with finger rolls, cooked sliced onion and tomato, and tomato ketchup and/or mustard.

100 g/4 oz white cabbage

100 g/4 oz red cabbage

2 large carrots

1 onion

25 g/1 oz sultanas

25 g/1 oz raisins

100 ml/3$\frac{1}{2}$ fl oz mayonnaise

2 tbsp lemon juice

salt and pepper

extremely easy — serves 4

Wash and shred the white and red cabbage. Grate the carrots, and finely chop the onion. Put all the prepared vegetables into a large salad bowl, then wash the sultanas and raisins and add them to the bowl.

In a separate bowl, mix together the mayonnaise and lemon juice, season with salt and pepper and pour over the salad. Mix all the ingredients together until well combined. Serve at once, or cover with clingfilm and refrigerate until ready to use.

mixed **cabbage** coleslaw

aubergine & mozzarella sandwiches

1 large aubergine

1 tbsp lemon juice

3 tbsp olive oil

salt and pepper

125 g/4$^{1}/_{2}$ oz grated mozzarella cheese

2 sun-dried tomatoes, chopped

Italian bread, mixed salad leaves and tomato slices
  to serve

very easy - serves 2

Preheat the barbecue. Using a sharp knife, slice the aubergine into thin rounds.

Mix the lemon juice and olive oil together in a small bowl and season the mixture with salt and pepper to taste. Brush the aubergine slices with the olive oil and lemon juice mixture and cook over medium hot coals for 2–3 minutes, without turning, until golden on the under side.

Turn half of the aubergine slices over and sprinkle with cheese and chopped sun-dried tomatoes.

Place the remaining aubergine slices on top of the cheese and tomatoes, turning them so that the pale side is uppermost. Barbecue for 1–2 minutes, then carefully turn the whole sandwich over and barbecue for a further 1–2 minutes. Baste with the olive oil mixture.

Serve with Italian bread, mixed salad leaves and a few slices of tomato.

spinach & orange salad

225 g/8 oz fresh baby spinach leaves

2 large oranges

1/2 red onion

DRESSING

3 tbsp extra-virgin olive oil

2 tbsp freshly squeezed orange juice

2 tsp lemon juice

1 tsp clear honey

1/2 tsp wholegrain mustard

salt and pepper

very easy - serves 4

Wash the spinach leaves under cold running water and dry them thoroughly on kitchen paper. Remove and discard any tough stalks and tear the larger leaves into smaller pieces.

Slice the top and bottom off each orange with a sharp knife, then remove the peel. Carefully slice between the membranes of the orange to remove the segments.

Using a sharp knife, finely chop the onion. Mix the salad leaves and orange segments together and arrange in a serving dish. Scatter the chopped onion over the salad.

To make the dressing, whisk the olive oil, orange juice, lemon juice, honey, mustard and salt and pepper to taste together in a small bowl. Pour the dressing over the salad just before serving. Toss the salad well to coat the leaves with the dressing.

avocado, sweetcorn & walnut salad

350 g/12 oz canned sweetcorn

75 g/3 oz walnuts, chopped

2 large, ripe avocados

6 tbsp lemon juice

6 tbsp soured cream

25 g/1 oz walnuts, chopped, to garnish

extremely easy - serves 4

Drain the sweetcorn, then put it into a large salad bowl. Add the walnuts and mix until well combined.

Peel, stone and cut the avocados into small pieces, brush them with some of the lemon juice to prevent discoloration, then add them to the salad.

In a separate bowl, mix the remaining lemon juice with the soured cream until a smooth consistency is reached. Add more lemon juice or cream if necessary. Add the lemon cream to the salad, stir it in, sprinkle with chopped walnuts, and serve.

650 g/1 lb 7 oz small new potatoes

125 g/4¹/₂ oz rocket leaves

150 g/5¹/₂ oz firm mozzarella

1 large pear

1 tbsp lemon juice

salt and pepper

DRESSING

3 tbsp extra-virgin olive oil

1¹/₂ tbsp white wine vinegar

1 tsp sugar

pinch of mustard powder

very easy — serves 4

Bring a saucepan of salted water to the boil. Add the potatoes, lower the heat and cook for about 15 minutes, until tender. Remove from the heat, drain and set aside to cool.

When the potatoes are cool, halve them and place them in a large salad bowl. Wash and drain the rocket leaves, cut the mozzarella into cubes, and wash, trim and slice the pear. Add them to the bowl along with the lemon juice. Season with salt and pepper.

To make the dressing, mix together the oil, vinegar, sugar and mustard powder. Pour the dressing over the salad and toss all the ingredients together until they are well coated. Serve at once.

potato, rocket & mozzarella salad

Something Sweet

Sweet treats, hot from the coals can provide the grand finale to your barbecue. Simplicity is the key with contemporary desserts that have an international flavour, such as Chocolate Rum Bananas or Barbecued Fruit with Maple Syrup.

chocolate rum bananas

1 tbsp butter
225 g/8 oz plain or milk chocolate
4 large bananas
2 tbsp rum

grated nutmeg, to decorate

crème fraîche, mascarpone cheese or
 ice cream, to serve

very easy - serves 4

Take four 25-cm/10-inch squares of aluminium foil and brush them with butter.

Cut the chocolate into very small pieces. Make a careful slit lengthways in the peel of each banana, and open just wide enough to insert the chocolate. Place the chocolate pieces inside the bananas, along their lengths, then close them up.

Wrap each stuffed banana in a square of foil, then barbecue them over hot coals for about 5–10 minutes, until the chocolate has melted inside the bananas. Remove from the barbecue, place the bananas on individual serving plates, and pour some rum into each banana. Serve at once with crème fraîche, mascarpone cheese or ice cream, topped with nutmeg.

4 apples, such as Granny Smiths

3 tbsp lemon juice

3 tbsp butter

4 tsp brown sugar

8 tbsp sweet mincemeat

natural yogurt, crème fraîche or mascarpone
cheese, to serve

easy - serves 4

Wash the apples, then cut them in half from top to bottom. Remove the cores and pips, then brush the cut sides of the apples with lemon juice to prevent discoloration.

Put the butter in a small saucepan and gently melt it over a low heat. Remove from the heat, then brush the cut sides of the apples with half of the butter. Reserve the rest of the melted butter.

Sprinkle the apples with sugar, then transfer them to the barbecue, cut sides down, and cook over hot coals for about 5 minutes. Brush the apples with the remaining butter, then turn them over. Add a tablespoon of mincemeat to the centre of each apple, then cook for another 5 minutes, or until they are cooked to your taste.

Remove from the heat and transfer to serving plates. Serve at once with natural yogurt, crème fraîche or mascarpone cheese.

barbecued apples

stuffed pears

2 tsp unsalted butter, for greasing

4 firm dessert pears

2 tbsp lemon juice

4 tbsp rosehip syrup

1 tsp green peppercorns, lightly crushed

140 g/5 oz redcurrants

4 tbsp caster sugar

ice cream, to serve

easy – serves 4

Preheat the barbecue. Cut out 4 squares of foil, each large enough to enclose the pears, and grease with the butter. Halve and core the pears, but do not peel. Brush the cut surfaces with lemon juice. Place 2 pear halves on each of the foil squares, brush them with the rosehip syrup and sprinkle with the peppercorns.

Place the redcurrants in a bowl and sprinkle with the sugar. Spoon the redcurrant mixture into the cavities of the pears. Fold up the sides of the foil to enclose the pears securely.

Cook over hot coals for 20 minutes. Serve immediately with ice cream.

fruit parcels

2 oranges

2 eating apples

juice of 1 lemon

2 pears

4 tsp muscovado sugar

very easy – serves 4

Preheat the barbecue. Peel the oranges, carefully removing all the pith. Cut each orange horizontally into 6 slices. Core the apples, but do not peel. Cut each apple horizontally into 6 slices. Brush the slices with lemon juice. Peel and core the pears, then cut each of them horizontally into 6 slices. Brush the slices with lemon juice.

Cut out 4 large squares of foil. Divide the fruit slices equally between the squares and sprinkle each pile with 1 teaspoon of the sugar. Fold up the sides of the squares to enclose the fruit securely.

Cook the parcels over medium hot coals for about 4 minutes. Serve immediately in the parcels.

toffee fruit kebabs

2 dessert apples, cored and cut into wedges

2 firm pears, cored and cut into wedges

juice of $\frac{1}{2}$ lemon

25 g/1 oz light muscovado sugar

$\frac{1}{4}$ tsp ground allspice

25 g/1 oz unsalted butter, melted

SAUCE

125 g/4$\frac{1}{2}$ oz butter

100 g/3$\frac{1}{2}$ oz light muscovado sugar

6 tbsp double cream

easy - serves 4

Preheat the barbecue. Toss the apple and pears in the lemon juice to prevent any discoloration.

Mix the sugar and allspice together and sprinkle over the fruit. Thread the fruit pieces onto skewers.

To make the toffee sauce, place the butter and sugar in a saucepan and heat, stirring gently, until the butter has melted and the sugar has dissolved.

Add the cream to the saucepan and bring to the boil. Boil for 1–2 minutes, then leave to cool slightly.

Meanwhile, place the fruit kebabs over hot coals and cook for 5 minutes, turning and basting frequently with the melted butter, until the fruit is just tender. Transfer the fruit kebabs to warmed serving plates and serve with the cooled toffee sauce.

4 large nectarines

200 g/7 oz frozen summer fruits (such as blueberries and raspberries), defrosted

3 tbsp lemon juice

3 tbsp honey

crème fraîche, mascarpone cheese or ice cream, to serve

very easy - serves 4

Cut out eight 18-cm/7-inch squares of aluminium foil. Wash the nectarines, cut them in half and remove the stones. Place each nectarine half on a square of foil.

Fill each nectarine half with summer fruits, then top each one with 1 teaspoon of lemon juice, then 1 teaspoon of honey.

Close the foil around each nectarine half to make a parcel, then barbecue them over hot coals for about 10–15 minutes, according to your taste. Remove from the barbecue, place the nectarines on serving plates and serve at once with crème fraîche, mascarpone cheese or ice cream.

summer **fruit** nectarines

barbecued fruit with maple syrup

1 papaya

1 mango, peeled and stoned

2 bananas

2 peaches, halved, stoned and peeled

1 ogen melon, halved and seeded

115 g/4 oz unsalted butter, diced

4 tbsp maple syrup

pinch of ground mixed spice

easy - serves 4

Preheat the barbecue. Cut out 4 large squares of foil. Thickly slice the mango and remove the stone, then peel off the skin and cut the flesh into slices. Using a sharp knife, cut the papaya in half and remove the seeds, then cut the halves into thick slices and peel off the skin. Peel the bananas and cut in half lengthways. Slice the peach halves. Cut the melon halves into thin wedges, then cut the flesh away from the rind. Divide the fruit between the foil squares.

Put the butter and maple syrup into a food processor and process until thoroughly blended and smooth. Divide the flavoured butter between the parcels of fruit and sprinkle with a little mixed spice. Fold up the sides of the foil to enclose the fruit securely.

Cook over medium hot coals, turning occasionally, for 10 minutes. Remove from the parcels and serve immediately.

cinnamon fruit with chocolate smoothie

4 slices fresh pineapple

2 kiwi fruit, peeled and quartered

12 strawberries, hulled

1 tbsp melted unsalted butter

1 tsp ground cinnamon

1 tbsp orange juice

SMOOTHIE

225 g/8 oz plain chocolate

25 g/1 oz unsalted butter

125 g/4$\frac{1}{2}$ oz caster sugar

125 ml/4 fl oz evaporated milk

1 tsp vanilla essence

4 tbsp Kahlúa

easy - serves 2

Preheat the barbecue. To make the smoothie, break the chocolate into pieces and melt with the butter in a saucepan over a low heat. Stir in the sugar and evaporated milk and cook, stirring, until the sugar has dissolved and the sauce has thickened. Transfer to a heatproof bowl and set on the side of the barbecue to keep hot.

Cut the pineapple slices into chunks. Thread the pineapple chunks, kiwi fruit and strawberries alternately onto several presoaked wooden skewers. Mix the butter, cinnamon and orange juice together in a small bowl. Brush the fruit kebabs all over with the cinnamon butter.

Cook the kebabs over hot coals, turning and brushing frequently with any remaining cinnamon butter, for 3–5 minutes, or until golden. Just before serving, stir the vanilla essence and Kahlúa into the smoothie.

1 pineapple
3 tbsp dark rum
2 tbsp muscovado sugar
1 tsp ground ginger
4 tbsp unsalted butter, melted

totally tropical pineapple

very easy - serves 4

Preheat the barbecue. Using a sharp knife, cut off the crown of the pineapple, then cut the fruit into 2-cm/³/₄-inch thick slices. Cut away the peel from each slice and flick out the 'eyes' with the point of the knife. Stamp out the cores with an apple corer or small pastry cutter.

Mix the rum, sugar, ginger and butter together in a jug, stirring constantly, until the sugar has dissolved. Brush the pineapple rings with the rum mixture.

Cook the pineapple rings over hot coals for 3–4 minutes on each side. Transfer to serving plates and serve immediately with the remaining rum mixture poured over them.

4 peaches

175 g/6 oz mascarpone cheese

40 g/1 1/2 oz pecan nuts or walnuts, chopped

1 tsp sunflower oil

4 tbsp maple syrup

very easy - serves 4

Cut the peaches in half and remove the stones. If you are preparing this recipe in advance, press the peach halves together and wrap in clingfilm until required.

Mix the mascarpone cheese and pecans together in a bowl until well combined. Leave to chill in the refrigerator until required.

Preheat the barbecue. Brush the peach halves with a little sunflower oil and place on a rack set over medium hot coals. Cook the peach halves for 5–10 minutes, turning once, until hot.

Transfer the peach halves to a serving dish and top with the mascarpone and nut mixture.

Drizzle the maple syrup over the peaches and mascarpone filling and serve immediately.

peaches with creamy mascarpone

INDEX